Drawings by Samuel Bu[...]
Text by Jean-Charles Volkmann

Agrégé d'histoire

100 Dates in French History

Translated by Angela Caldwell

Editions Jean-Paul Gisserot

www.editions-gisserot.com

About 15,000 BC:
Decoration of the cave in
Lascaux.
Prehistoric Man develops
cave art. The Lascaux cave
is situated in Dordogne.

About 4,500 BC: Erection of dolmens and standing stones.
During the Stone Age, people become sedentary and society is
based on farming. People erect dolmens bury their dead.

-52 BC: Gallic chieftain,
Vercingetorix, surrenders to
Julius Caesar in Alesia.
The Romans complete their
conquest of Gaul. A Gallo-
Roman civilisation develops,
marked by the construction
of many large buildings.

177: Persecution of the Christians. The martyrdom of St Blandine in Lyon.

From the 2nd century, Christianity begins to spread through the Roman Empire. Christians are subjected to widespread attack by the Roman Emperors and the persecution of St Blandine in 177 A.D is particularly severe. At the end of the 4th century, St Martin, Bishop of Tours, spreads Christianity throughout Gaul.

732 A.D.: Charles Martel stops the Saracens in Poitiers.
After the conquest of the Iberian Peninsula (Spain), the Saracens launch attacks on Gaul. Charles Martel, Mayor of the Palace, stops them in Poitiers. Although he is not the monarch, Charles really rules the country when the Merovingian dinasty is in decline, during the era of the "Idle Kings".

About 498 A.D.: Baptism of Clovis, King of the Franks.
The Roman Empire collapses as a result of Barbarian invasions. Several different tribes, among them the Franks, settle in France. Clovis becomes their King in about 481 A.D. and conquers the whole country. He founds the Merovingian dynasty.

778 A.D.: Death of Roland in Roncesvalles during one of Charlemagne's campaigns in Spain.
Charlemagne, who has been King of the Franks since 768 A.D.and founder of the Carolingian dynasty, conquers huge territories. It is during an expedition in Spain in 778 A.D. that Charlemagne's nephew, Roland, is killed fighting a skirmish in the mountain pass in Roncesvalles.

800 A.D.: Charlemagne is crowned Emperor in Rome by the Pope.
Charlemagne goes to Rome in 800 A.D. to save Pope Leo III who crowns him Emperor on 25th. December.

885-886 A.D.: The Viking Siege of Paris.
The Franks have to fight invasions by the Vikings, Norsesem who sail up the rivers in their flat-bottomed longships. Paris is plundered several times. To put an end to this threat, King Charles III the Simple grants the Vikings territory of Normandy.

987 A.D.: Hugh Capet is elected King of France.
On 3rd, July 987, the country's leading noble-men elect a lord from the Paris Basin, Hugh Capet, to the throne of France. This marks the beginning of rule by the Capetians the dynasty, that really founds the country of France.

Mid 11th Century – mid 12th century: Construction of Romanesque churches.
Mediaeval society is, deeply religious, building cathedrals in an architectural style that reflects the economic and cultural development of the western world from the 11th century onwards.

1096: The start of the Crusades.
For about two centuries, Christians fight to recapture the Holy Places, that are in Moslems hands. There are eight Crusades in all, ending in 1270.

1137: Marriage of King Louis VII and Eleanor of Aquitaine.

One of the ways the Kings of France extend their hold over the kingdom is by marriages. When Louis VII marries Eleanor of Aquitaine, he obtains the entire South West of the country. They divorce in 1152. When Eleanor remarries with the future King of England, she bring as her dowry half the western part of the kingdom. This leads to a struggle between France and England lasting several hundred years.

Mid 12th century: The introduction of Gothic architecture.

From the mid 12th century, Romanesque architecture is succeeded by the Gothic style, creating much larger churches. The most famous are the cathedrals in Chartres, Reims and Paris (Notre-Dame).

1214: King Philip Augustus wins the Battle of Bouvines.

This victory of French King Philip Augustus on 27th July, 1214 over a coalition led by the German Emperor Frederick II, is the first expression of French nationalist feeling.

1226: Accession of King Louis IX (St. Louis).

St. Louis' reign (1226-1270) is marked by a will to maintain law and order in the kingdom. The king is a very pious man, taking part in the last two Crusades, to win back the Holy Places.

1307: King Philip the Fair arrests the Knights Templar.
The kingdom's financial difficulties lead King Philip the Fair to attack the Knights Templar, in an attempt to zeize their, wealth. The Knights Templar are arrested, sentenced and executed in 1310.

1309: The Popes settle in Avignon.
Leaving Italian quarrels, behind him, the French born Pope, Clement V moves to Avignon in 1309 and for more than half a century, the Christian Church is run from this town in the South-East of France where the Popes have a sumptuous palace built.

1346: The English army defeats the French at Crecy.
This is the first great battle of the Hundred Years' War and, during it, the French cavalry is routed. For the French, this is a bad start to their struggle against the English.

1347 – 1352: Major Black Death epidemic throughout the country.
After suffering a succession of military defeats, France falls prey to the epidemic of Black Death which has already spread from Asia Minor. The Black Death, or, plague, reaps havoc throughout Western Europe for six years. Whole regions are devastated, especially in the South of the Kingdom.

1356: King John II the Good is defeated in Poitiers and imprisoned in London.
The Hundred Years' War is still being fought. In Poitiers, John II the Good is captured and taken to London. He does not return to his kingdom until July 1360. During those four years, the country is run by John the Good's eldest son, Charles.

1364: Du Guesclin defeats the Spaniards at Cocherel.
Bertrand du Guesclin, a great mediaeval warrior, is in the service of the King of France. He defeats the King of Navarre, Charles the Bad, at the Battle of Cocherel in 1364. He is then successful in fighting the English, chasing them out of the West and the South-West of the kingdom.

1392: King Charles VI becomes insane.
Having reigned over France since 1380, Charles VI suffers his first attack of insanity in 1392 while riding thought the forest on the outskirts of Le Mans. This is the beginning of a very difficult era which lasts until the death of the King in 1422.

1407: The assassination of the Duke of Orléans and the beginning of civil war between Armagnacs and Burgundians.
King Charles VI's insanity leads to a struggle for power between the Dukes of Orléans and Burgundy. Rivalry between the two men results in the murder of the King's brother, Duke Louis of Orléans by men in the service of John the Fearless, Duke of Burgundy. His death leads to civil war between supporters of the Armagnacs and the Burgundian factions.

1415: The French army is routed by the English at Azincourt.
When the new English King, Henry V, lands in France, war begins again between the two countries leading to a new disaster for the French cavalry which loses 10,000 men at the Battle of Azincourt.

1431: Death of Joan of Arc.
The young shepherdess from Domrémy is called by God to save France, and the country is gradually retaken by the French under King Charles VII. Joan of Arc is captured and handed over to the English. She is sentenced and burnt at the stake in Rouen.

1453: French victory at Castillon-la-Bataille. End of the Hundred Years' War.
Since the 1430's, King Charles VII of France has gained the upper hand over the English. This decisive victory allows him to recapture Guyenne, in the South-West of the country.

1461: Accession of King Louis XI.
Louis XI takes advantage of the law and order brought to the kingdom by his father, Charles VII, Louis XI and continues to improve the country's finances and legal system. However, he is best remembered for building the country we know as France. To do it, Louis XI fights against great feudal noble-men, especially the Duke of Burgundy, Charles the Bold.

1477: Death of Charles the Bold, Duke of Burgundy, during the Siege of Nancy.
Charles the Bold, the last of the kingdom's great feudal noblemen, becomes Duke of Burgundy in 1477 and remains King Louis XI of France's worst enemy. Their power struggle lasts ten years and only ends when Charles dies.

1491: Marriage of King Charles VIII and Anne of Brittany.

François II, the last Duke of Brittany, dies in 1488 after having tried to preserve Breton independence. Defeated by the royal troops, he is obliged to accept the conditions laid down by Charles VIII, who marries Anne, heiress to the duchy, in 1491. This marriage paves the way for the annexation of Brittany to France.

1494: Beginning of the Italian wars with King Charles VIII.

In love with adventure and crusades, young King of France Charles VIII, answering favourably the call of the Pope against the King of Naples, launches into an expedition in Italy. After victories, all the conquests are lost in 1496-1497. This defeat marks the end of the Italian dream of Charles VIII, who dies in 1498.

Late 15th century – mid 16th century: Construction of the Loire Valley castles. Introduction of the Renaissance to France.

The intellectual, scientific and artistic movement known as "the Renaissance" appears in Italy during the 14th century, and reaches France as a result of the "Italian Campaign". King François I invites Leonardo da Vinci to Court. The most outstanding reminders of the new era are the castles in Chambord, Blois and Chenonceaux.

1515: Accession of King François I. French victory at Marignano.
François I, who becomes King at the age of 20, is the archetypal Renaissance knight, fond of both fighting and the Arts. As soon as he mounts the Throne, he resumes the Italian campaign and wins the Battle of Marignano, This allows him to take the Milan area.

1524: Death of Bayard the Knight at the Battle of Sesia in Italy.
Bayard the Knight is a symbol of the Renaissance warrior, a model of bravery and respect for the enemy; he is known as the "fearless and blameless Knight". He plays a part in many victories but is killed during the wars of François I.

1525: King François I is defeated at Pavia in Italy. He is taken captive and imprisoned in Madrid.
Ten years after his victory at Marignano, King François I again does battle in Italy in his struggle against Emperor Charles V. Defeated in Pavia, he is taken captive and held in Spain until March 1526, after the signature of the Treaty of Madrid and the payment of a huge ransom.

1534: The "placards" affair. Spread of the Reformed Religion. François I's reign is marked by the spread of Protestantism throughout the Kingdom. Tolerated by the King for a long time, the "Heretics" are persecuted after the "placards" affair when ; pamphlets supporting Lutheran ideas are displayed in several towns in which the Court is resident.

1534: Jacques Cartier explores Canada. Jacques Cartier, a sailor from Saint-Malo in Brittany, reaches Newfoundland and then explores the St Lawrence River during several expeditions from 1534 onwards. He takes possession of the land he discover on behalf of King François I but the Royal government considers his conquests to be of little interest gives up any plans for settlement.

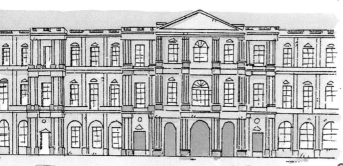

1546: François I launches the construction of a new Louvre palace. The Louvre was originally a fortified castle built by King Philip Augustus at the end of the 12th century. Charles V extended it in the 14th century. The Louvre Palace is demolished during the reign of François I, who commissions architect Pierre Lescot to draw up the plans for a new modern palace. Work on the new building begins during the second half of the 16th century.

1559: Death of King Henri II. During a tournament organised to celebrate the marriage of his daughter, Elizabeth, with King Philip II of Spain, the Count of Montgomery fatally wounds the King of France in the eye.

1572:
Massacre of the Protestants on St Bartholomew's Day.
Since 1562, France has been ravaged by war between Catholics and Protestants. The bloodiest episode of the Wars of Religiontakes place on 24th August, 1572 when thee thousand pleople are murdered. This is known as the St Bartholomew's Day Massacre.

1589: Assassination of King Henri III.
Henri III, who has been King since 1574, is unable to put an end to the Wars of Religion and the prospect of Protestant King Henri de Navarre mounting the throne revives the war between Catholics and Protestants. On 1st August 1589, a fanatical monk named, Jacques Clément murders King Henri III, who has been driven out of by a riot Paris in May 1588.

1593: King Henri IV converts to Roman Catholicism.
Although recognised as heir to the Throne by Henri III, Henri IV is only considered as King by the Protestants. He realises that the only thing preventing him from being accepted as king by everybody in France is his religion so he abjures Protestantism on 25th July, 1593 in the St Denis basilica and becomes a Roman Catholic.

1598: Edict of Nantes. End of the Wars of Religion.
King Henri IV wins the country ovr agai-nis mainly through the return of religious tolerance. The French are tired of conflic and long for peace. The King's signature of the Edict of Nantes on 13th, April 1598 marks the end of the Wars of Religion, and gives the Protestants free-dom of worship.

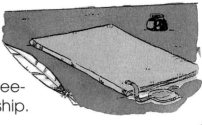

1610: Assassination of King Henri IV, by Ravaillac.
Despite his restoration of religious peace and royal authority, Henri IV is hated throughout his reign by uncompromising Catholics and he has to foil many plots and murder attempts. He is assassinated on 14th May, 1610 in the heart of Paris by a fanatic named Ravaillac.

1624: Richelieu becomes King Louis XIII's Prime Minister.
After being kept under the thumb of his mother, Marie de Medici, and her favourites, Louis XIII calls in Cardinal Richelieu. This is the beginning of eighteen years of collaboration between the two men and Richelieu eventually holds all the power in his own hand.

1627-1628: Royal troops lay siege to the Protestant town of La Rochelle.
Richelieu wants to reverse the privileged situation that the Protestants have enjoyed since the Edict of Nantes. The town of La Rochelle symbolises their power and Louis XIII decides to attack it. After a siege lasting for more than a year, Richelieu seizes the town. Its population has been decimated by famine.

1635: King Louis XIII founds the French Academy.
The "Académie Française", set up at Richelieu's request in January 1635, is the oldest and most prestigious of the academies. Its purpose is to uphold the purity of the French language. The King becomes the protector of the Arts and Letters.

1643: Accession of King Louis XIV, Mazarin becomes Prime Minister.
King Louis XIII is succeeded by a five-year old child, Louis XIV. His mother, Anne of Austria, becomes Regent, but it is Cardinal Mazarin who rules the country until 1661 working to build a system of absolute monarchy.

1648-1653: The "Fronde", a Parliamentary and aristocratic uprising against Mazarin's power.
This parliamentary and aristocratic uprising is the last violent demonstration against the system of absolute monarchy symbolised by Mazarin. Even though royal power emerges as the winner after this serious crisis, it has a profound effect on the young King Louis XIV.

1661: Arrest of Nicolas Fouquet, Superintendent of Finances.
At the very beginning of his personal reign, Louis XIV orders the arrest of Nicolas Fouquet, Superintendent of Finances. The King of France cannot tolerate the power of his minister, who has a castle in Vaux-le-Vicomte and who has amassed huge wealth. After a rigged trial, Fouquet is imprisoned in the Pignerol Fortress until his death in 1680.

1665: Colbert becomes Controller General of Finances.
Having served as a minister since 1662, Jean-Baptiste Colbert is appointed Controller General of Finances by Louis XIV in 1665. He becomes the most important and most influential of all the ministers until his death in 1683. Among other things, he sets up a Navy designed for war.

1679: Vauban begins the construction of his system of fortifications.
Appointed Commissioner General of Fortifications by King Louis XIV, Vauban repairs or builds more than three hundred fortified towns round the kingdom's borders ensuring the defence of the country in case of foreign invasion.

1681: Louis XIV seizes the city of Strasbourg.
Military victories won during the War of Devolution (against the Spaniards) and the Dutch war urge Louis XIV to annex areas along the North-Eastern borders of the country in order to protect the kingdom from attack. During this period, Louis XIV enters the city of Strasbourg and formally takes to possession of it.

1682: King Louis XIV moves to the Palace of Versailles.

The Palace of Versailles symbolises absolute monarchy and reflects the greatness and power of the "Sun King". It is the largest architectural project undertaken during the reign of Louis XIV. The King turns a hunting lodge into a huge palace and moves there with his the Court. Luxury, excess, receptions and celebrations are the main features of Court life during his reign and that of his successors.

1685: Revocation of the Edict of Nantes, Resumption of persecutions of the Protestants.

Louis XIV wants to restore the religious unity of the country an end to Protestantism, a religion that has been accepted since 1598. The Revocation of the Edict of Nantes is the final example of anti-Protestant action taken since the 1660's. Several thousands of Protestants leave the country while others continue to worship in secret.

1709: Major famine and misery in the country.

The whole 17th century and the early 18th century are marked by the regular recurrence of crises during which people do not have even the basic necessities of life. Poor harvests caused by bad weather lead to famine, high death rates and appalling misery. The crisis in 1709 is the last of the major crises before the French Revolution.

1715 : Death of King Louis XIV, Accession of Louis XV, his great-grandson.
King Louis XIV dies on 1st September, 1715, after a reign of 72 years. His successor is his great-grandson, Louis XV, aged 5, his only living descendant. Philippe of Orleans, Louis XIV's nephew, becomes the country's regent.

1745: Madame de Pompadour, King Louis XV's mistress.
Throughout his reign, Louis XV, who is not really interested in affairs of State, leaves power to his ministers and influenced by his many mistresses. The Marquise de Pompadour is the most important of them all. She plays a major role at the Court of Versailles Court from 1745 to 1764, tarnishing the King's image.

1774: Accession of King Louis XVI.
Louis XVI succeeds his grandfather, Louis XV, at the age of twenty. In a country profoundly influen-ced by the ideas of the "Age of Enlightenment", subject to serious financial difficulties and whose image of Monarchy is deteriorated, the young King, despite his good intentions, is not the man or the job.

1777: General La Fayette fights in America with the American rebels. Beginning of the French struggle against the English.
The Declaration of Independence signed by the thirteen American colonies on 4th July 1776 leads to a war against England. This "wind of freedom" excites a few French gentlemen such as La Fayette who goes to the United-States in1777 to fight by the side of the American rebels.

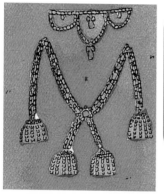

1785-1786: The affair of Queen Marie-Antoinette's necklace.
This famous swindle involving Marie-Antoinette casts even more discredit on the French monarchy in general and the reign of Louis XVI in particular. Although innocent, the Queen is criticised for her ill-considered expenses, at a time when the kingdom's finances have grown weaker. The affair puts the finishing touch to the Queen's unpopularity.

1789: Beginning of the French Revolution with the Meeting of the States General.
The financial crisis, economic and social problems and opposition within Parliament finally lead the King to convene the States General. The French people draw up books of complaints to let the King know of their difficulties and concerns. They elect their representatives. This is the beginning of the French Revolution.

1789: Storming of the Bastille.
This event remains the most famous and most symbolic of all the events that took place during the French Revolution. Parisians look for arms and gunpowder to defend themselves, worried by the dismissal of Necker and by the arrival of troops. The Bastille fortress, a symbol of the absolute monarchy is stormed by the people on 14th July. This date become France's national bank holiday in 1880.

1792: French victory in Valmy against the Austrians and the Prussians.

The heroic and symbolic victory of the young revolutionary army near the mill in Valmy on 20th September saves France and the Republic. The French army then takes the initiative and begins a war aimed at the conquest of new territory.

1793: Execution of King Louis XVI.

Louis XVI's double dealings since the beginning of the Revolution and his secret negotiations with foreign sovereigns lead to his arrest and trial. Sentenced to death, Louis XVI shows exemplary courage when he goes to the guillotine on 21st January 1793.

1793: Assassination of Marat.

The assassination of one of the great revolutionary figures in his bath by a young royalist from Normandy named Charlotte Corday, is one of the best known episodes in the French Revolution.

1794: Robespierre establishes the Reign of Terror.

The Montagnards party seizes power in June 1793 and, inherits a disastrous situation. The Revolution is being threatened from inside and outside the country. They resort to terror to redress the situation Robespierre gradually establishes a dictatorship and tens of thousands of suspects are executed in 1794.

1796: Victory of General Bonaparte in Italy at the Arcole Bridge.
Young General Bonaparte wins brilliant victories at the head of an army sent to Italy to fight against Austria. His popularity increases after the victory at the Arcole Bridge on 17th November 1796, when he fights his way across the river at the head of his soldiers.

1798: Expedition of General Bonaparte in Egypt. Battle of the Pyramids.
As part of its struggle against England, the Government sends Bonaparte to conquer Egypt. This expedition in a country which fascinates Bonaparte, brings him a hero's reputation, thanks to victory reports sent to France.

1804: Bonaparte becomes Emperor under the name of Napoleon I.
After being in power since November 1799 with the title of First Consul, Bonaparte establishes an Empire in May 1804. Pope Pius VII comes to Paris for the Coronation of Napoleon I on 2nd December in Notre Dame Cathedral.

1805: Victory of Napoleon I over Russians and the Austrians in Austerlitz.
Of all the battles fought by Napoleon I, the one that takes places in Austerlitz on 2nd December 1805, on the anniversary of the imperial coronation, remains a remarkable example of military strategy. The Emperor of the French wins an outstanding victory over the Russians and the Austrians.

1812: Retreat from Russia, passage of the Beresina River.
After the breakdown of the alliance with Russia, Napoleon I sets up a huge army to attack the country. In spite of the capture of Moscow, the Russian army remains undefeated and Napoleon decides to withdraw. The crossing of the Beresina River in November is the most tragic moment in the retreat, with the loss of half-a-million men.

1815: Defeat of Napoleon I at Waterloo and abdication. Exile on St Helena.
Waterloo represents the last battle and the final defeat of Emperor Napoleon I by the English and the Prussians. He abdicates for the second time and is deported to the Island of St. Helena in the Southern Atlantic where he dies in 1821.

1830: Beginning of the conquest of Algeria by the French.

The capture of Algiers marks the resumption of French colonial conquests after the loss of the country's original Empire in the 18th century. However, is takes several decades to complete the military conquest of Algeria. In particular, the struggle against Abd-el Kader lasts until 1847.

1830: The "Three Glorious Days" in Paris. Overthrow of King Charles X.

King Charles X, the last representative of the Bourbon royal family, governs as an absolute monarch, increasing the unpopularity of the system. The publication of measures restricting civil liberties leads to a popular uprising in Paris. Three days of revolution lead to the abdication of Charles X.

1840 years: Beginning of the Industrial Revolution.
France progressively enters the industrial era during the reign of Louis-Philippe I.
Factories are built, coal is mined on a massive scale, railway lines start to cover the country, agriculture is modernised and society undergoes change.

1848: King Louis-Philippe I is overthrown by a revolution. Proclamation of the Second Republic.
The economic and social changes resulting from the Industrial Revolution worsen the conditions of workers and increase discontent. The 1847 economic crisis and the lack any real slackening of the political reins under Louis-Philippe I lead to another revolution, putting an end to the monarchy in France once and for all.

1852: The President of the Republic, Louis-Napoleon Bonaparte, establishes the Empire and becomes Napoleon III.
Having been President of the Republic since 1848, Louis-Napoleon Bonaparte holds all power after the coup of 2nd December 1851. One year later, he proclaims the Second Empire and takes the title Napoleon III.

1870: War against Prussia. Fall of the Second Empire. Proclamation of the Third Republic. France loses Alsace and Lorraine through the Treaty of Frankfurt.
Napoleon III launches a policy of confrontation against Prussia and this leads to war in 1870. The French army is quickly defeated and the Emperor is forced to abdicate. A Republic is proclaimed and the new government signs the Treaty of Frankfurt, which gives Germany Alsace and part of Lorraine.

1871: The Paris Commune.
During the Franco-Prussian War of 1870, Paris is besieged by the Prussians. Surrender brings with it a feeling of humiliation among the people of Paris who rebel and set up a "Commune". The government under President Thiers retakes the city and the Paris Commune ends with a week of bloodshed..

1881-1882: Jules Ferry's laws institute secular, free mandatory primary education.
This politician of the Third Republic has given his name to one of the major achievements of the new government. The access to free, non-religious instruction for everybody provides learning for successive generations of young people who, in turn, provide the best possible support for the Republican system.

1885: Pasteur develops the first rabies vaccination.
A biologist named, Louis Pasteur becames famous for the first experimental rabies vaccination on the young Joseph Meister. His fight to find a method of immunisation against disease makes him one of the great pioneers of medical advances in the 19th century.

1889: Construction of the Eiffel Tower for the World Fair in Paris.
This monument, which is one of the most famous in the French capital city, shows the importance of steel at the end of the 19th century. The Eiffel Tower is built for the World Fair.

1894: The Dreyfus affair. The officer is pardoned in 1899 and reinstated in 1906.
Captain Dreyfus, a French army officer, is suspected of spying for Germany and is sentenced to be deported. This leads to a serious political and judicial crisis. President Loubet eventually pardons Dreyfus, once his innocence has been proven. However, Dreyfus is not reinstated as a major in the Army until 1906.

1895: The Lumière brothers invent the cinematograph.

In an era of increasingly rapid technical and scientific progress, the Lumière brothers, Louis and Auguste, create what becomes known as "cinema" because the cinematograph was developed thanks to the work of these two scientists.

1905: The law separating the Church and the State.
President Emile Combes radical government introduces more and more anticlerical measures from 1902 and, in 1904, diplomatic relations are broken off with the Pope. The final affect of this policy is a law separating the Church and the State, making France a non-religious country.

1909: Louis Blériot flies across the Channel.
The first aeroplanes are built in the early years of the 20th century but there are many failures before any real flights are made Blériot's crossing of the Channel is one of the first success stories in the history of flying.

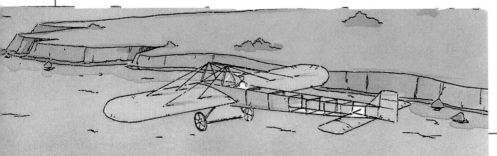

1914-1918: First World War. Battle of Verdun in 1916.

The assassination of Archduke Franz Ferdinand, heir to the Throne of Austria-Hungary, on 28th June 1914 in Sarajevo plunges Europe into a terrible war that costs many human lives. The Battle of Verdun in 1916 is the best example of this huge loss of life.

1931: Colonial exhibition in Vincennes.

In the 1930's the French Colonial Empire is at its peak. France is present on all the continents, from Africa to Indochina, and, from the West Indies to the islands of the Pacific. The 1931 Colonial Exhibition, illustrates this world-wide influence.

1936: The Popular Front wins the elections. Social reforms and paid holidays.

The left-wing parties, united under the name of "Popular Front", win the general election in 1936. A Socialist, Léon Blum, becomes the Head of Government. Social reforms are introduced (working week reduced to 40 hours, two weeks' paid holiday every year).

1940: Second World War. General De Gaulle sends out an appeal from London.
Attacked by Germany in May 1940, the French army collapses, leading to the fall of the Third Republic. Maréchal Pétain signs the Armistice and sets up the French State in Vichy, which begins to collaborate with Germany. General De Gaulle flees to London and calls upon the French people to resist the Occupation in a radio message broadcast on 18th June.

1944: Allied landings in Normandy.
After occupying France for four years, Germany's stranglehold on Europe is brought to a close by the Allied landings on the Coast of Normandy on 6th June. This marks the beginning of the liberation of France which is completed in a few weeks. In August, General De Gaulle sets up a temporary government in Paris.

1947-1958: Fourth Republic. Reconstruction of the country.
After the end of the war, the setting up of new institutions is a long and difficult task. The Fourth Republic does not come into being until January 1947. Faced with economic and social difficulties linked to the reconstruction of the country and to colonial issue the new regime weakens quickly and collapses after eleven years.

1946-1954: War of Indochina.

War breaks out after the proclamation of Vietnamese independence by Communist leader Hô Chi Minh. The Vietnamese, who receive help from China, take advantage of the terrain and use guerrilla tactics. As a result they quickly defeat the French army which is forced to capitulate at Dien Ben Phu in 1954. The Geneva Accords grant independance to French Indochina.

1957: Treaty of Rome, creating the European Economic Community.

After the Second World War that left Western Europe severely weakened, the idea of reconciliation between countries gain ground. The Treaty of Rome sets up the European Economic Community (EEC) between six countries: France, Italy, the Federal Republic of Germany, Belgium, Luxembourg and the Netherlands.

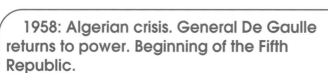

1958: Algerian crisis. General De Gaulle returns to power. Beginning of the Fifth Republic.

Colonial issues lead to the fall of the Fourth Republic. A military coup in Algiers brings General De Gaulle back to power of. He introduces a new constitution that sets up the Fifth Republic. De Gaulle becomes its first president in January 1959.

1962: Independence of Algeria. French settlers have to leave the country. From 1959 onwards, General De Gaulle gradually works towards the independence of Algeria. The signature of the Evian Accords on 18th March 1962 puts an end to the war and to the French presence in the country. About one million Europeans who lived in the country return to France, leaving all their possessions behind.

1968: Student unrest and social crisis. De Gaulle resigns in 1969.
After being in power, for ten years, General De Gaulle is facted with serious student unrest and a social crisis in 1968. Though he successfully overcomes it, as proven by the landslide victory of his supporters in the general election, his hold on power is fatally weakened The failure of the 1969 referendum and his resignation are the consequences of this situation.

1981-1995: François Mitterrand, President of the Republic.

François Mitterrand is elected in 1981, then re-elected in 1988, ying in office for two seven-year terms. Setting aside the political changes and the economic and social difficulties, the main hievement of this period is the continuation of the move towards a more ted Europe through the Treaty of Maastricht. Mitterrand also wants to leave an architectural reminder of his presidency, through the Louvre Pyramid, the Bastille Opéra House, the Grande Arche de La Défense and the National Library of France in Paris.

1995-2002 : from 7 year presidential terms to 5 year terms. Political changes.

In September 2000, a referendum shortened the length of presidential terms from 7 to 5 years. Jacques Chirac (for his second term between 2002 and 2007), followed by Nicolas Sarkozy (2007-2012), are the first presidents to experiment the five year presidential term. France is then to face several political changes the right governs from 1995 to 1997, followed by a period of « cohabitation » between 1997 and 2002 with Jacques Chirac appointing socialist Lionel Jospin as his Prime Minister following a parliamentary elections setback. Then, the right returns from 2002 until 2012: re-elected Presiden Jacques Chirac appoints Jean-Pierre Raffarin a his Prime Minister in 2002 then replaces him with Dominique de Villepin in 2005 ; President Nicola Sarkozy appoints François Fillon as his Prime Minister in 2007. During this period, France enter the Third Millennium and keeps integrating ever more in the European Union in spite of a majority of French voters answering « no » in a referendum on the ratification of a European Constitution in 2005. The Euro currency is introduced in 2002. Economically, France is marred by a financial crisis from 2008 on, weighed by a tremendously high level of public spending and an abysmal public debt. In 2012, after new elections, François Hollande becomes the new French President.

IMPRIM'VERT® Updating : April 2014

© 2000 - 2014 Editions GISSEROT PARIS
Printed by Pollina 85400 Luçon N° L68245
Printed in France